Making Choices
at SCHOOL

By Diane Lindsey Reeves

21st Century
Junior Library

Published in the United States of America by
Cherry Lake Publishing
Ann Arbor, Michigan
www.cherrylakepublishing.com

Reading Adviser: Marla Conn MS. Ed., Literacy specialist, Read-Ability, Inc.

Photo Credits: Cover, © Pressmaster; page 4, © Monkey Business Images; page 6, © wavebreakmedia; page 8, © wavebreakmedia; page 10, © Poznyakov; page 12, © Tyler Olson; page 14, © wakebreakmedia; page 16, © Ivonne Wierink; page 18, © Olga Enger; page 20, © Monkey Business Images. *Source: Shutterstock.*

Library of Congress Cataloging-in-Publication Data
Names: Reeves, Diane Lindsey, 1959- author.
Title: Making choices at school / by Diane Lindsey Reeves.
Description: Ann Arbor, Mich. : Cherry Lake Publishing, 2018. | Series: Smart choices |
    Includes bibliographical references and index. | Audience: K to Grade 3.
Identifiers: LCCN 2017035918| ISBN 9781534107854 (hardcover) |
    ISBN 9781534109834 (pdf) | ISBN 9781534108844 (pbk.) | ISBN 9781534120822
    (hosted ebook)
Subjects: LCSH: Schools—Juvenile literature. | School day—Juvenile literature. |
    School environment—Juvenile literature. | Choice (Psychology)—Juvenile literature. |
    Decision making—Juvenile literature.
Classification: LCC LB1513 .R44 2018 | DDC 371.01—dc23
LC record available at https://lccn.loc.gov/2017035918

Cherry Lake Publishing would like to acknowledge the work of The Partnership for 21st Century Skills.
Please visit *www.p21.org* for more information.

Printed in the United States of America.

CONTENTS

5 **Back to School**

11 **New Things to Learn**

17 **Taking a Break**

22 My Smart Choices

23 Glossary

24 Index

24 About the Author

Quick! It's time for school to start.

Back to School

You get to school just as the bell rings loudly. Brring! You're glad you got here on time. You didn't want to be **tardy**.

This is your chance to learn all you can. There will be lessons and stories. Then recess and lunch. You get to spend time with friends.

In this book, you will make choices. Think of ways you can be a good student.

My Choice!

- Be on time and ready to learn
- Be tardy and unprepared

There are good reasons for **rules** like raising hands in class.

You find your seat. The class quiets down. Remember the rules? Rules make things go smoothly. They tell us how to **behave**.

There is a time to be quiet. There is a time to talk. Walk, don't run. Raise your hand to ask questions. Be nice to your friends.

What kind of rules do you have in your class? Are you quick to **obey** them?

My Choice!

- Obey the rules and have a good day
- Go against the rules and get into trouble

It is fun to help with classroom **chores**.

Everyone says, "Good morning!" Then it is time to begin. Your teacher will lead you through the morning **routine**. There's roll call and the pledge to the flag. Then there are chores to get done.

What is your favorite job to do? Every job is important. You learn **responsibility**. And it helps out your teacher a lot.

My Choice!

- Pitch in and help with classroom chores
- Refuse to do your classroom chores

Special classes like art make learning fun.

New Things to Learn

Put on your thinking cap! Which subject comes first? Is it reading or writing? Maybe some math?

Art and music classes add extra fun. You can find helpful books in the library. You work out your wiggles in PE.

Will you do your best work? It is your choice!

My Choice!

- Listen and do my best
- Goof off and cause trouble

Someone has run out of **energy** today.

Learning takes effort. There is listening to do. There are problems to solve. Stories to write. Projects to work on.

It helps when you are rested. Your brain can think better. Eating good food gives you energy. Be sure to sip water. It helps keep you **alert**.

What kinds of healthy choices do you make? Do they help you learn better?

My Choice!

- Make healthy choices
- Forget to take good care of my body

Working on teams is a good way to learn.

Working together on projects makes learning fun. It is teamwork. Everyone pitches in. Everyone shares ideas. Everyone learns from each other.

Teams work best when everyone does their part. It is not fair when people don't help. It is no fun when people get bossy.

Can your team count on you?

My Choice!

- Do my part for the team
- Let other people do all the work

Time for lunch!

Taking a Break

Going to the **cafeteria** is a nice break. There's time to eat. And time to visit with friends. Don't be too loud! The lunch lady will **scold** you.

Do you bring a lunch from home? Or do you buy it at school? Do you eat healthy foods? Or do you fill up on snacks?

Good choices give you energy to learn.

My Choice!

- Eat a good lunch and enjoy my friends
- Eat unhealthy food and make too much noise

Recess!

Is **recess** a favorite part of your day? There is a lot to like about going outside. All that fresh air. Friends to play with. Getting exercise and goofing off.

Recess lets you enjoy some free time. Running around and playing are good for your brain!

Do you play nicely at recess? Are you kind to all the kids in your class?

My Choice!

- Play nicely with others
- Boss the other kids around

School is out. It's time to go home.

The last bell rings. It is time to go home. After all your hard work, it is time for a break. You are smarter now than you were this morning.

Gather your things together. Do you walk home? Do you ride a bus? Does a parent pick you up? Be safe getting home!

Did you make good choices at school today?

My Choice!

- I am happy with the choices I made today
- I need to make better choices tomorrow

MY SMART CHOICES

Write a story about two different days. One day you make smart choices at school. The other day you don't. How are the two days different? Which day did you enjoy the most?

GLOSSARY

alert (uh-LURT) paying attention to what is around you and ready to act

behave (bih-HAYV) to act in a polite and proper way

cafeteria (kaf-uh-TEER-ee-uh) a room in a school where meals are served and eaten

chores (CHORZ) jobs that have to be done regularly

energy (EN-ur-jee) the strength to do things without getting tired

obey (oh-BAY) to do what you are told to do

recess (REE-ses) a break from schoolwork in the morning or afternoon

responsibility (rih-spahn-suh-BIL-ih-tee) a duty or a job

routine (roo-TEEN) a regular order of doing things

rules (ROOLZ) official instructions for conduct or action

scold (SKOHLD) to tell someone in an angry way that he or she has done something wrong

tardy (TAHR-dee) late, not on time

INDEX

A

art class, 11

C

cafeteria, 17
chores, 8, 9

E

effort, 13

L

library, 11

M

math, 11
music class, 11
My Choice, 5, 7,
    9, 11, 13, 15, 17,
    18, 21
My Smart Choices,
    22

P

PE, 11

R

reading, 11
recess, 19
rules, 6, 7

T

tardy, 5
teams, 14, 15

W

writing, 11

ABOUT THE AUTHOR

When Diane Lindsey Reeves isn't writing children's books, she chooses to play with her four grandchildren. She lives in Cary, North Carolina, and Washington, D.C.